The Ope

A219 Exploring the Classical World

Illustrations Book

This publication forms part of an Open University course A219 Exploring the Classical World. Details of this and other Open University courses can be obtained from the Student Registration and Enquiry Service, The Open University, PO Box 197, Milton Keynes, MK7 6BJ, United Kingdom: tel. +44 (0)870 333 4340, email general-enquiries@open.ac.uk

Alternatively, you may visit the Open University website at http://www.open.ac.uk where you can learn more about the wide range of courses and packs offered at all levels by The Open University.

To purchase a selection of Open University course materials visit http://www.ouw.co.uk, or contact Open University Worldwide, Michael Young Building, Walton Hall, Milton Keynes MK7 6AA, United Kingdom for a brochure. tel. +44 (0)1908 858785; fax +44 (0)1908 858787; email ouwenq@open.ac.uk

The Open University

Walton Hall, Milton Keynes

MK7 6AA

First published 2009.

Edited and designed by The Open University.

Typeset by The Open University.

Printed and bound in the United Kingdom by Nicholson & Bass Ltd.

ISBN 978 1 8487 3199 8

1.1

Colour Plate 1 Athens: Acropolis. Parthenon, west front 447–438 BCE (width 31m; height 14m). © The Open University. Photo: James Robson.

Colour Plate 2 Athens: Acropolis. Parthenon, detail of north-east corner. Metope 447–439 BCE; pediment sculpture 440–432 BCE. © The Open University. Photo: James Robson.

Colour Plate 3 Temple of Poseidon, Cape Sounion. Fifth century BCE. ©1990, Photo: Scala, Florence.

Colour Plate 4 Temple of Hera II (so-called Temple of Neptune), Paestum. © 1990, Photo: Scala, Florence. Courtesy of the Ministero Beni e Attività Culturali.

Colour Plate 5 Athens: Acropolis. The Propylaea, east front. 437–432 BCE. © 1990, Photo: Scala, Florence.

Colour Plate 6 Athens: Parthenon. Fragment of cornice showing traces of paint. (Overall dimensions 35 x 53cm; depth of meander band 17.1cm.) BM Cat. Sculpture 358, British Museum, London. © Copyright The Trustees of the British Museum.

Colour Plate 7 Athens: Parthenon. Plaster cast of cornice block with reconstruction of painted decoration. (Overall dimensions 35 x 48cm; depth of meander band 18 cm.) BM Cat. Sculpture 358, British Museum, London. © Copyright The Trustees of the British Museum.

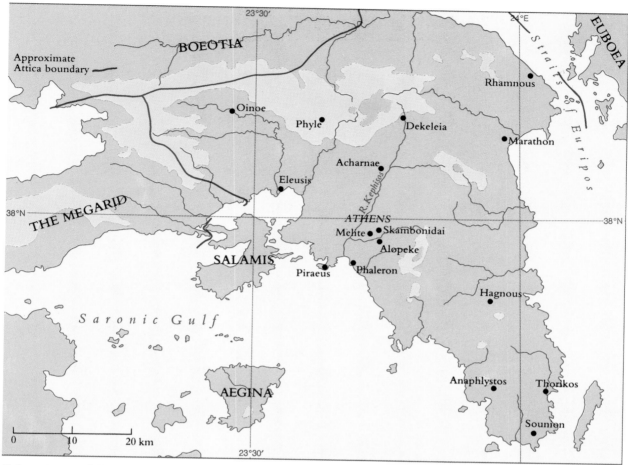

Colour Plate 8 Map of Attica. © The Open University.

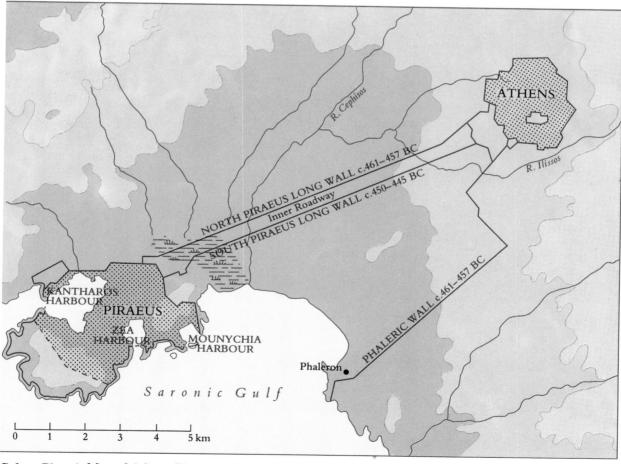

Colour Plate 9 Map of Athens, Piraeus and the Long Walls. © The Open University.

Colour Plate 10 *Ostrakon* bearing the name 'Cimon son of Miltiades'. Pieces of inscribed pottery such as these were used to vote for the ostracism of prominent citizens at the Athenian Assembly. If over 6,000 votes for ostracism were cast in any one year, the man whose name appeared on the most *ostraka* was banished from Athens for ten years – a fate which befell Cimon in 461 BCE. Kerameikos Museum, Athens. © The Open University. Photo: James Robson.

Colour Plate 11 Sir Lawrence Alma-Tadema (1836–1912), *Pheidias and the Frieze of the Parthenon, Athens*, 1868, oil on panel. Birmingham Museums and Art Gallery. © The Bridgeman Art Library, London.

Colour Plate 12 Short side of the so-called altar of Domitius Ahenobarbus showing Neptune and Amphitrite, late second century BCE. Staatliche Antikensammlungen und Glyptothek, Munich. Photo: Staatliche Antikensammlungen und Glyptothek, Munich.

Colour Plate 13 Short side of the so-called altar of Domitius Ahenobarbus showing Nereids, Triton, and sea dragon, late second century BCE. Munich Glyptothek/Antikensammlung. Photo: Staatliche Antikensammlungen und Glyptothek, Munich.

Colour Plate 14 Long side of the so-called altar of Domitius Ahenobarbus showing a sacrifice by a censor, late second century BCE. Louvre, Paris. Photo: © RMN/© Les frères Chuzeville.

Colour Plate 15 Long side of the so-called altar of Domitius Ahenobarbus showing a sea thiassos and the marriage, late second century BCE. Staatliche Antikensammlungen und Glyptothek, Munich. Photo: Staatliche Antikensammlungen und Glyptothek, Munich.

Colour Plate 16 Idyllic pastoral scene with *sacellum* (little temple) *c*.10 BCE. Museo Nazionale, Naples. © 2004, Photo: Scala, Florence.

Colour Plate 17 Mosaic of gladiatorial combat, third century CE. Found near Rome. National Archaeology Museum, Madrid. Photographic Archive National Archaeology Museum, Madrid, inv. 2545.

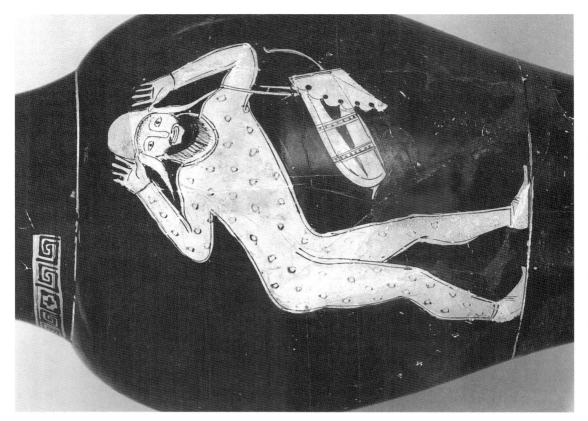

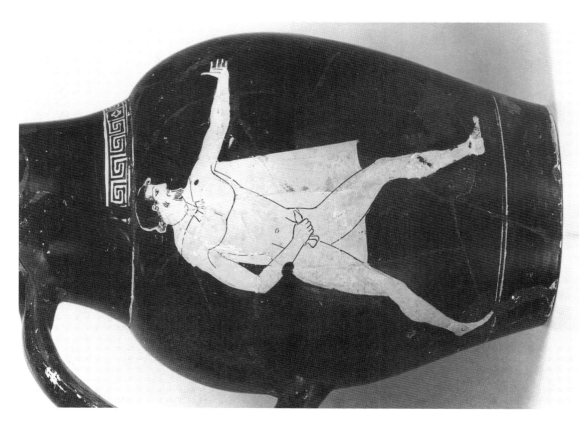

Plates 1 and 2 Two sides of an Athenian vase, dated *c.*460 BCE, possibly commemorating the battle of the Eurymedon. Museum für Kunst und Gewerbe, Hamburg.

Plate 3 Athens: Acropolis from the north west, Hymettos mountain range behind. Alison Franz Collection, American School of Classical Studies at Athens.

Plate 4 Athens: Acropolis. Reconstructed model based on the work of G.P. Stevens. With permission of the Royal Ontario Museum, Toronto. © ROM.

a) Heraion, Olympia, *c.*470–460 BCE

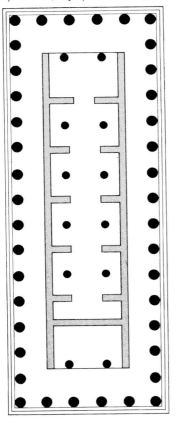

b) Temple of Apollo, Bassae, *c.*430–420 BCE

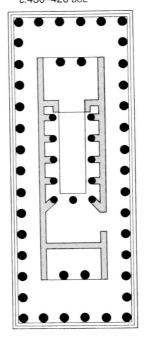

c) Temple of Aphaea, Aegina, *c.*475 BCE

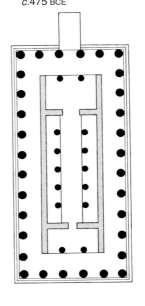

d) Temple at Segesta, Sicily, late fifth century BCE

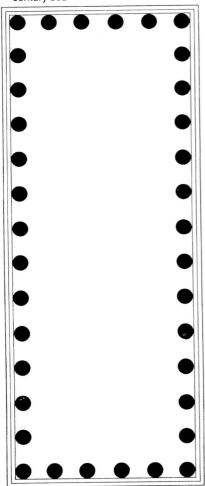

e) Temple of Hera II or Apollo, Paestum, *c.*474–460 BCE

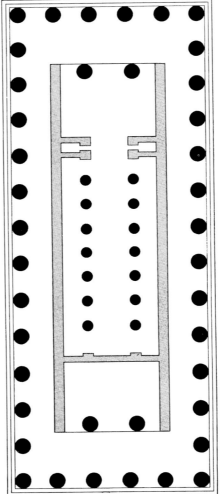

f) Temple B, Selinous, Sicily, third to second century BCE

g) Temple Athena Nike, Athens, Acropolis, *c.*425 BCE

h) Temple on the Ilissos, Athens, mid-fifth century BCE

Plate 5 Comparative plans of Greek temples drawn to scale. © The Open University.

i) Temple of Themis,
Rhamnous, early fifth
century BCE

j) Temple of Athena, Sounion,
south and east colonnade,
mid-fith century BCE

k) Temple of Hephaestus,
Athens, c.449–444 BCE

l) Temple of Poseidon,
Sounion, c.440 BCE

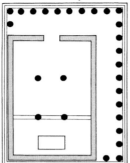

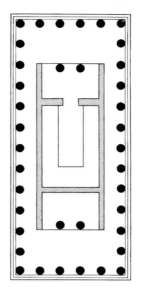

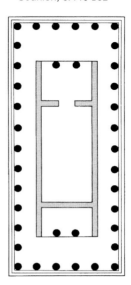

m) Temple of Zeus, Olympia, c.470–457 BCE

n) Parthenon, Athens, Acropolis, c.447–438 BCE

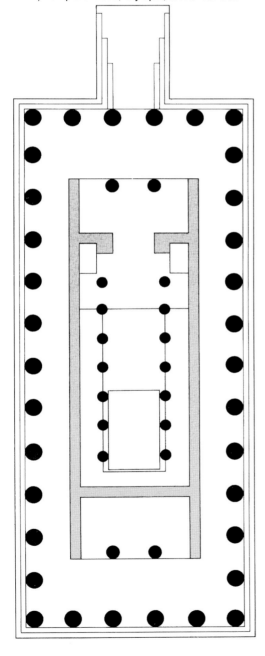

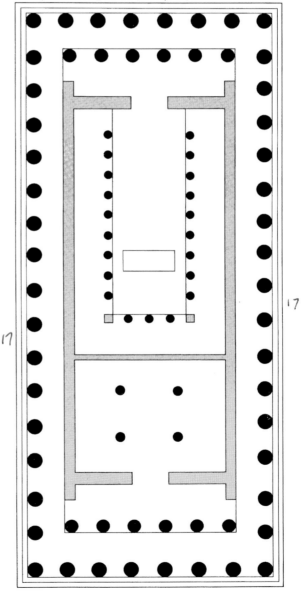

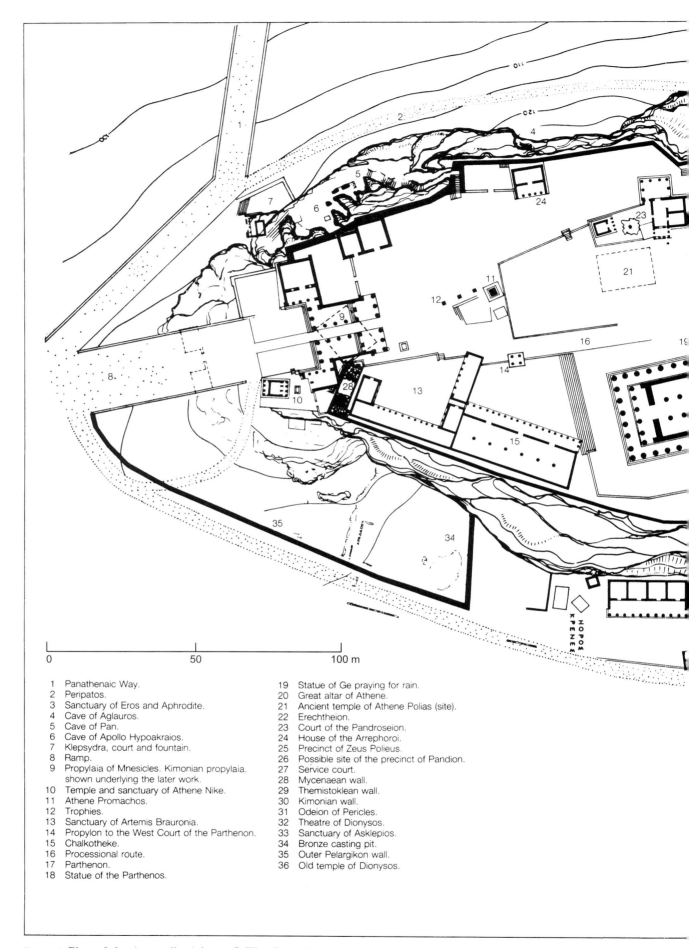

Plate 6 Plan of the Acropolis, Athens. © The Open University.

0   50   100 m

1   Panathenaic Way.
2   Peripatos.
3   Sanctuary of Eros and Aphrodite.
4   Cave of Aglauros.
5   Cave of Pan.
6   Cave of Apollo Hypoakraios.
7   Klepsydra, court and fountain.
8   Ramp.
9   Propylaia of Mnesicles. Kimonian propylaia.
    shown underlying the later work.
10 Temple and sanctuary of Athene Nike.
11 Athene Promachos.
12 Trophies.
13 Sanctuary of Artemis Brauronia.
14 Propylon to the West Court of the Parthenon.
15 Chalkotheke.
16 Processional route.
17 Parthenon.
18 Statue of the Parthenos.

19 Statue of Ge praying for rain.
20 Great altar of Athene.
21 Ancient temple of Athene Polias (site).
22 Erechtheion.
23 Court of the Pandroseion.
24 House of the Arrephoroi.
25 Precinct of Zeus Polieus.
26 Possible site of the precinct of Pandion.
27 Service court.
28 Mycenaean wall.
29 Themistoklean wall.
30 Kimonian wall.
31 Odeion of Pericles.
32 Theatre of Dionysos.
33 Sanctuary of Asklepios.
34 Bronze casting pit.
35 Outer Pelargikon wall.
36 Old temple of Dionysos.

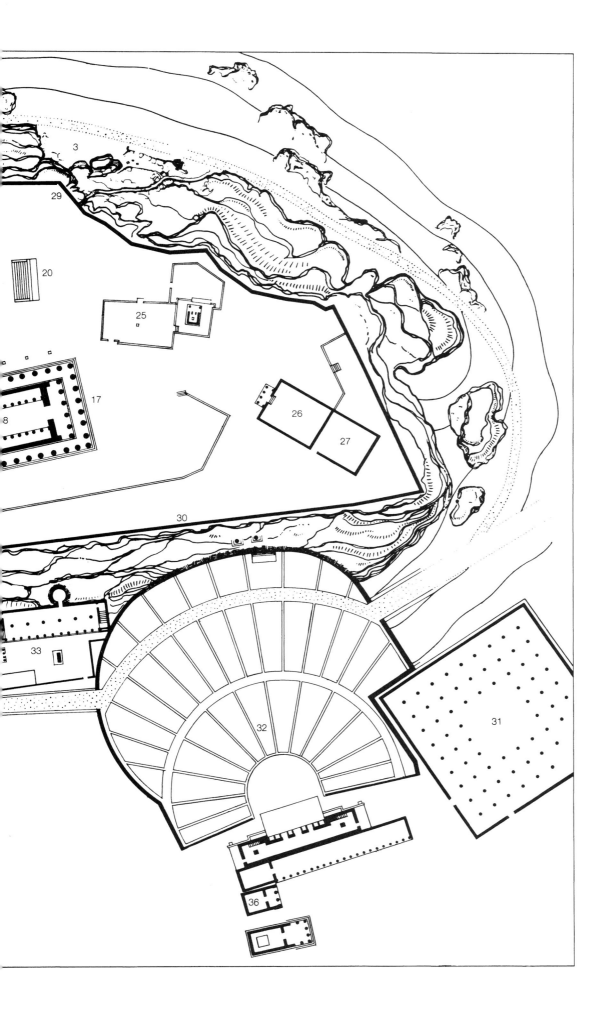

Plate 7 Athens: Hephaisteion, *c*.449–444 BCE (13.7 x 31.77m). American School of Classical Studies at Athens, Agora excavations.

Plate 8 Bassae: Temple of Apollo, *c*.430–420 BCE (15 x 38m). Hirmer Fotoarchiv, Munich.

Plate 9 Façade of the Temple of Athena Nike, fifth century BCE, rebuilt 1835. Acropolis, Athens. © Index/The Bridgeman Art Library, London.

Plate 10 Athens: Acropolis. Drawing of view from the Propylaea, with the gate wall removed. American School of Classical Studies at Athens, Agora excavations.

Plate 11 Athens: Parthenon. Reconstructed model of Athena Parthenos statue (height *c*.12m). With permission of the Royal Ontario Museum, Toronto. © ROM.

Plate 12 Athena Parthenos (the 'Varvakeion Athena'). Marble. Roman copy of gold-ivory fifth-century original by Phidias (*c*.500–432 BCE). National Archaeological Museum, Athens. © The Bridgeman Art Library, London.

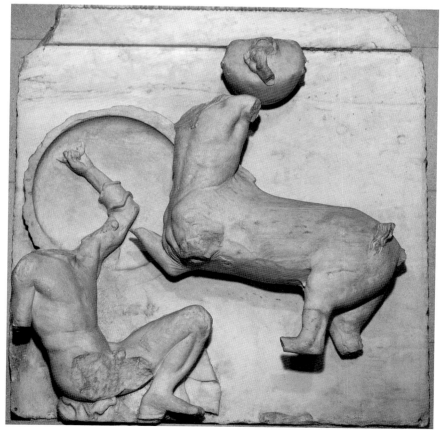

Plate 13 Athens: Parthenon. South metope IV. Lapith and centaur. 447–439 BCE (1.3 x 1.3m). © The Open University. Photo: Manuel Vason.

Plate 14 Athens: Parthenon. South metope III. Lapith and centaur. 447–439 BCE (1.3 x 1.3m). © The Open University. Photo: Manuel Vason.

Plate 15 Athens: Parthenon. South metope XXVII. Lapith and centaur. 447–439 BCE (1.3 x 1.3m). Athens: Parthenon. British Museum. © Copyright The Trustees of the British Museum.

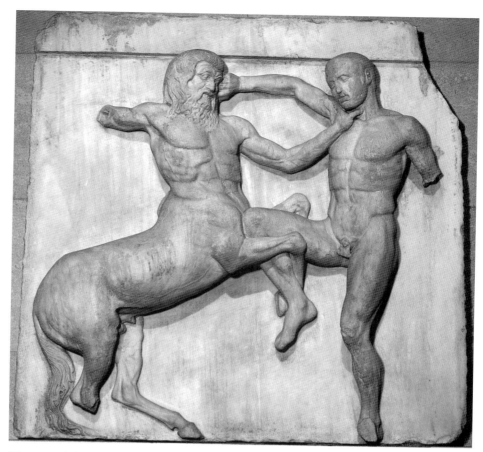

Plate 16 Athens: Parthenon. South metope XXXI. Lapith and centaur. 447–439 BCE (1.3 x 1.3m). © The Open University. Photo: Manuel Vason.

Plate 17 Athens: Parthenon. South metope XXVII. Lapith and centaur. 447–439 BCE (1.3 x 1.3m). © The Open University. Photo: Manuel Vason.

Plate 18 Athens: Acropolis. Reconstructed drawing from the west court of the Parthenon by G.P. Stevens. American School of Classical Studies at Athens, Agora excavations.

Plate 19 Athens: Acropolis. Parthenon, from the north west. © The Open University.
Photo: James Robson.

Plate 20 Athens: Acropolis. The Propylaea (437–432 BCE), looking north east from the Nike bastion.
Hirmer Fotoarchiv, Munich.

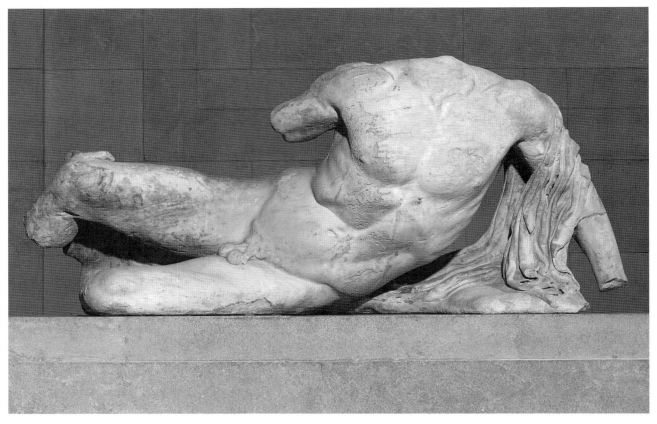

Plate 21 Athens: Parthenon. West pediment. Figure of a river god (Ilissos). 440–432 BCE. © The Open University. Photo: Manuel Vason.

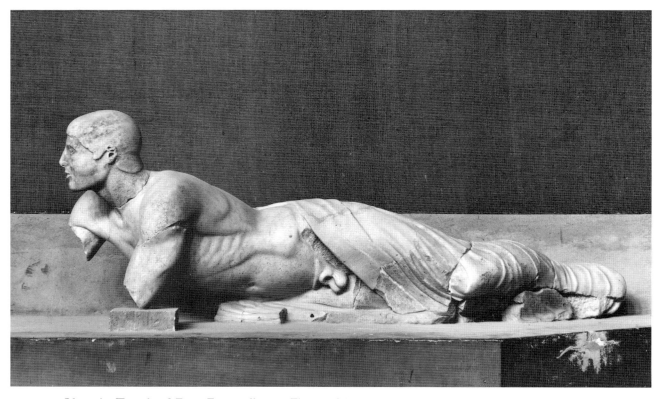

Plate 22 Olympia: Temple of Zeus. East pediment. Figure of Kladeos. 465–457 BCE. Hirmer Fotoarchiv, Munich.

Plate 23 Olympia: Temple of Zeus. Metope 10 with Heracles supporting the vault of the Sky, 465–464 BCE. Olympia Museum. © 1990, Photo: Scala, Florence.

Plate 24 Athens: Parthenon. East pediment. Three seated goddesses (Hestia, Dione, Aphrodite), 440–432 BCE. © The Open University. Photo: Manuel Vason.

Plate 25 Athens: Parthenon. West pediment. Figure of Iris, originally winged, 440–432 BCE. © The Open University. Photo: Manuel Vason.

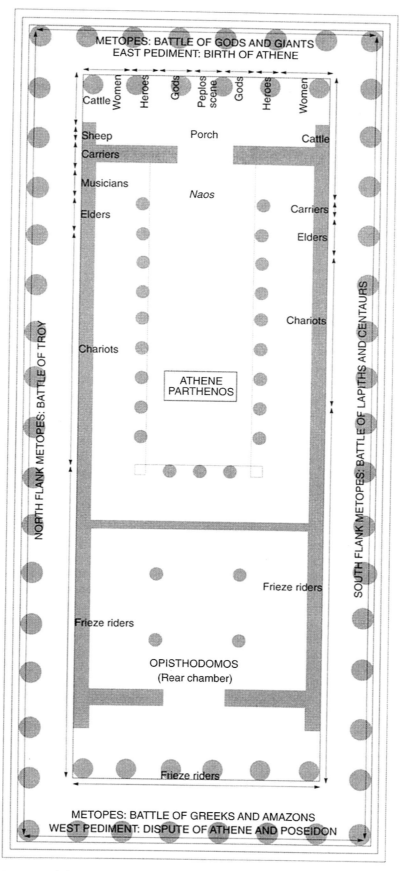

Plate 26 Athens: Parthenon. Plan showing the arrangement of the frieze and the metopes. © The Open University.

Plate 27 Athens: Parthenon. North frieze XVII. Standing figure and charioteer, *c*.442–438 BCE. © The Open University. Photo: Manuel Vason.

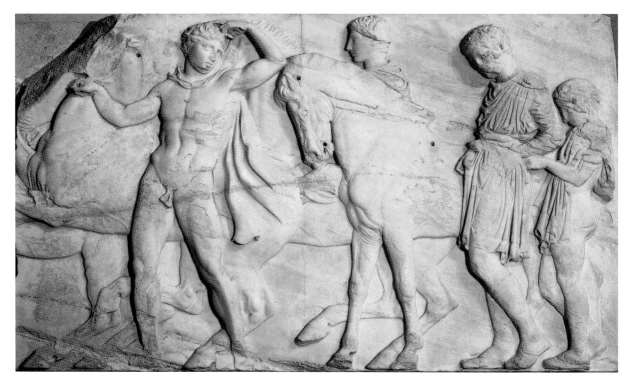

Plate 28 Athens: Parthenon. North frieze XLII. Horsemen preparing to start in procession, 442–438 BCE. © The Open University. Photo: Manuel Vason.

Plate 29 Athens: Parthenon. South frieze XXX. Charioteer, 442–438 BCE. © The Open University. Photo: Manuel Vason.

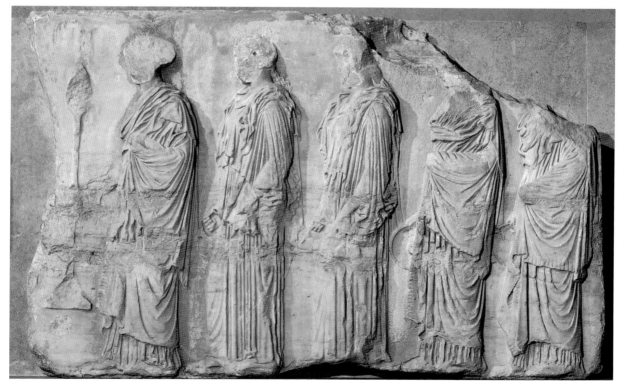

Plate 30 Athens: Parthenon. East frieze VIII. Girls carrying various items, 442–438 BCE. © The Open University. Photo: Manuel Vason.

Plate 31 Athens: Parthenon. North frieze XLI–XLIV. Horsemen, 442–438 BCE. © The Open University. Photo: Manuel Vason.

Plate 32 Athens: Parthenon. East frieze IV–VI, 442–438 BCE. © The Open University. Photo: Manuel Vason.

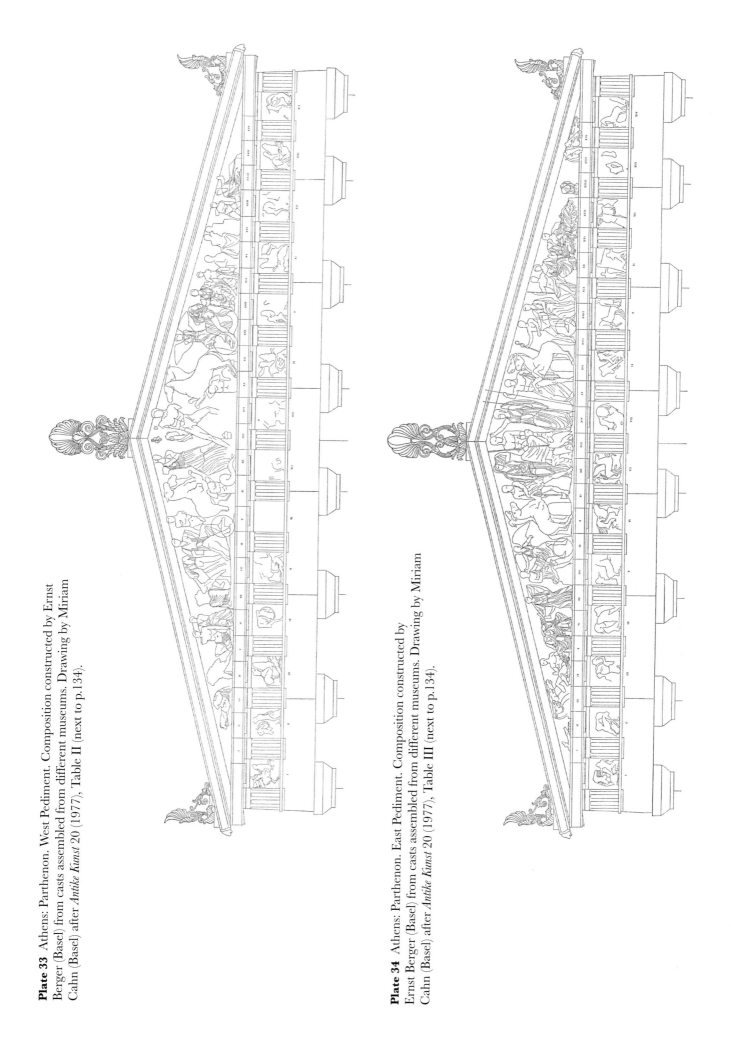

Plate 33 Athens: Parthenon. West Pediment. Composition constructed by Ernst Berger (Basel) from casts assembled from different museums. Drawing by Miriam Cahn (Basel) after *Antike Kunst* 20 (1977), Table II (next to p.134).

Plate 34 Athens: Parthenon. East Pediment. Composition constructed by Ernst Berger (Basel) from casts assembled from different museums. Drawing by Miriam Cahn (Basel) after *Antike Kunst* 20 (1977), Table III (next to p.134).

Plate 36 Aerial view of Paestum, 1943–45, from John Bradford, *Ancient Landscapes: Studies in Field Archaeology,* London: G. Bell & Sons, 1957, plate 52.

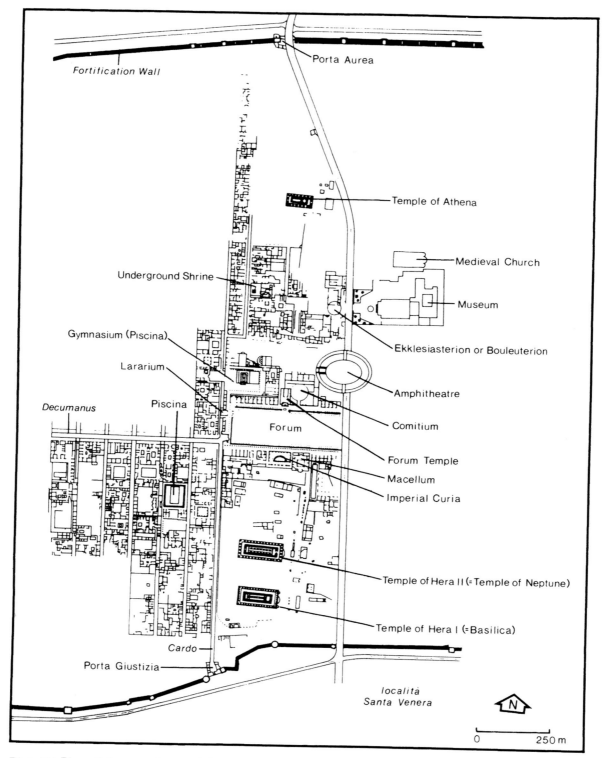

Plate 37 Plan of the central area of Paestum showing excavated remains and modern buildings, from John Griffiths Pedley, *Paestum: Greeks and Romans in Southern Italy*, London: Thames & Hudson, 1990, p.13. Note that the temple labelled as 'Hera II' is now thought to be dedicated to Apollo.

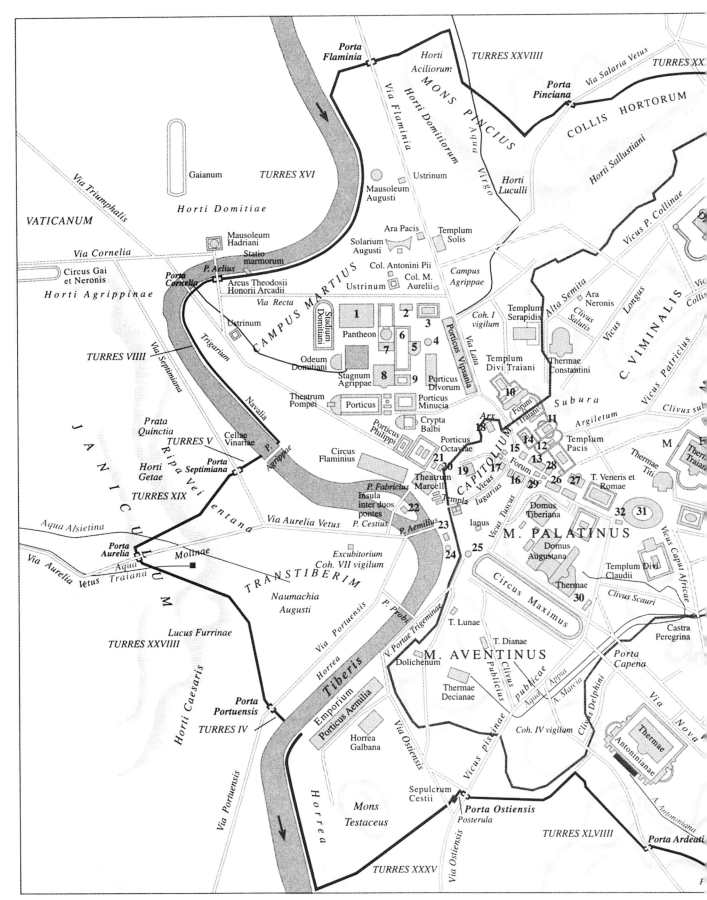

Plate 38 Map of the city of Rome, fourth century CE, from Eva Margareta Steinby, *Lexicon Topographicum Urbis Romae*, volume terzo, Edizioni Quasar, 1996, fig. 190, p.484. Note also the inner circuit of the 'Servian Walls' and the outer Aurelian Walls.

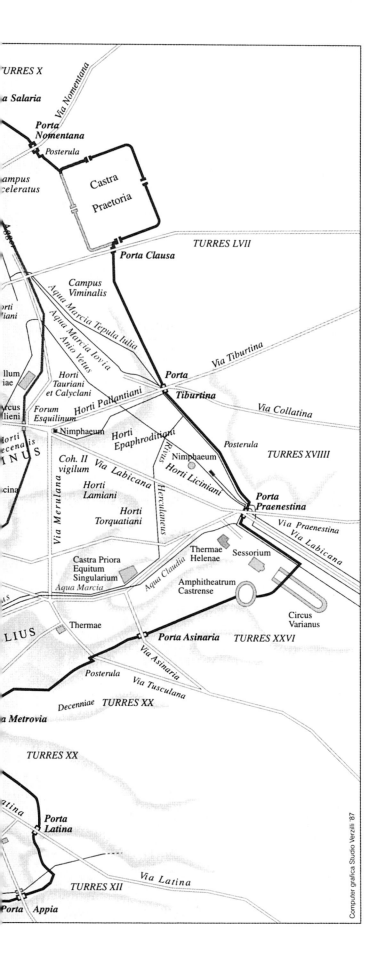

1 Baths of Nero

2 Temple of Matidia

3 Temple of the Divine Hadrian

4 Temple of Minerva

5 Serapeum

6 Saepta

7 Basilica of Neptune

8 Baths of Agrippa

9 Diribitorium

10 Trajan's Column

11 Forum of Augustus

12 Forum Transitorium

13 Basilica Aemilia

14 Forum of Julius Caesar

15 Arch of Septimius Severus

16 Basilica Julia

17 Temple of Saturn

18 Temple of Juno Moneta

19 Temple of Jupiter Optimus Maximus Capitolinus

20 Temple of Bellona

21 Temple of Apollo Medicus Sosianus

22 Temple of Aesculapius

23 Temple of Portunus

24 Temple of Hercules Olivarius

25 Temple of Hercules Aemilianus

26 House of the Vestal Virgins

27 Basilica of Constantine

28 Temple of Antoninus Pius and Faustina

29 Temple of Castor and Pollux

30 Septizodium

31 Colosseum

32 Arch of Constantine

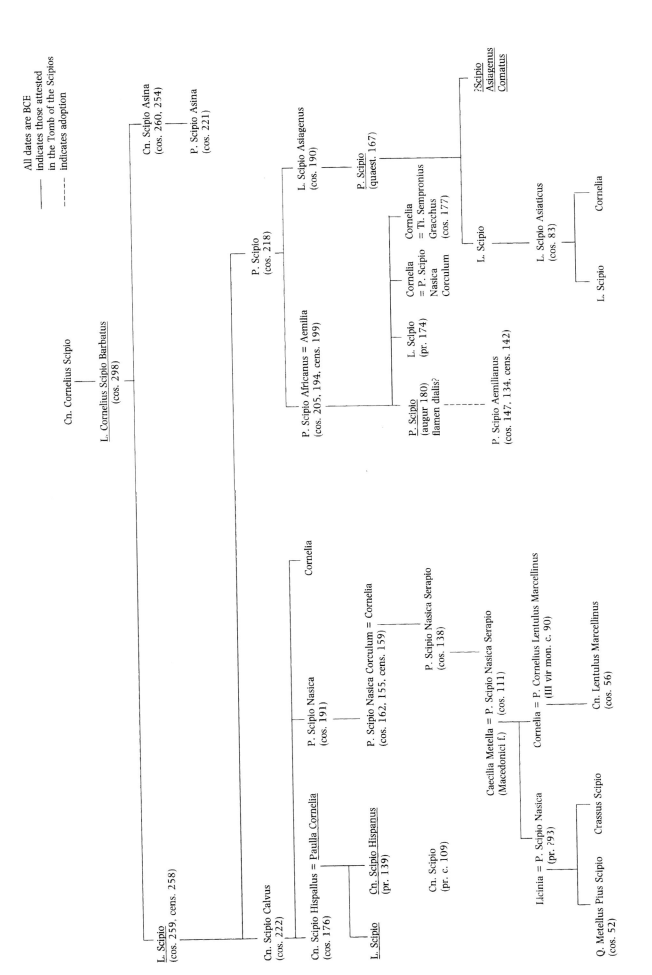

All dates are BCE

—— indicates those attested in the Tomb of the Scipios

----- indicates adoption

Plate 39 Family tree of the Cornelii Scipiones, from Harriet I. Flower, *Ancestor Masks and Aristocratic Power in Roman Culture*, Oxford: Clarendon Press, 1996, pp.356–57.

Plate 40 Statue of a Roman citizen holding two portrait busts of his ancestors, height 165cm, Palazzo dei Conservatori, Rome. Photo: Alinari Archives–Anderson Archive, Florence. Probably of Augustan date, end of first century BCE. The head on the statue itself is not original.

Plate 41 Bronze statue of Lupa Romana, Palazzo dei Conservatori, Rome, *c.*fifth century BCE.
Photo: Alinari Archives–Brogi Archive, Florence. The twins were added between CE 1471 and 1509.

Plate 42 Marble portrait head of Pompey the Great, height 25cm, *c.*50 BCE. Photo: Ny Carlsberg Glyptotek, Copenhagen. Probably a later (mid first century CE) copy of an original.

Plate 43 Statue of Augustus from the villa of Livia at Prima Porta, Rome. Vatican Museum, Rome, Braccio Nuovo, inv. 2290. Photo: Alinari Archives, Florence.

Plate 44 Detail of the breastplate of the statue of Augustus from the villa of Livia at Prima Porta, Rome, showing a Parthian handing back a legionary standard to a Roman. Vatican Museum, Rome, Braccio Nuovo inv. 2290. Photo: Alinari Archives, Florence.

Plate 45 Plan of the Isola Sacra Necropolis, Portus, near Ostia, from Henner von Hesberg and Paul Zanker (eds.), *Römische Gräberstrassen: Selbstdarstellung – Status – Standard: Kolloquium in München vom 28. bis 30. Oktober 1985*, Munich, 1987. Verlag der Bayerischen Akademie der Wissenschaften.

ЄM86

Plate 46 Relief panel from a tomb, depicting a chariot race, Gregorian Profane Museum, Vatican Museums. Photo: Alinari Archives–Anderson Archive, Florence.

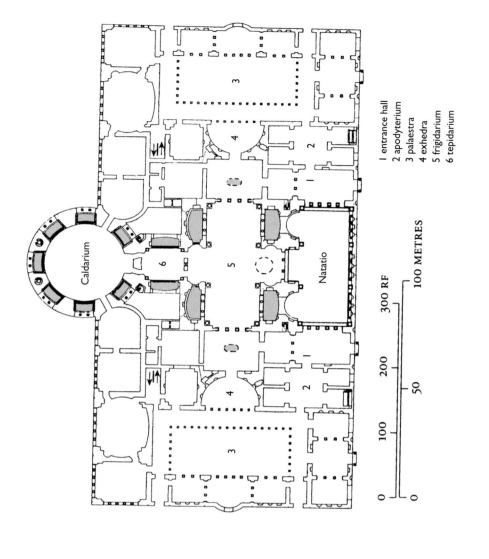

Plate 48 Central bath block of the Baths of Caracalla, reproduced from Amanda Claridge, *Rome-Oxford Archaeological Guide* (Oxford, OUP 1998).

1 entrance hall
2 apodyterium
3 palaestra
4 exhedra
5 frigidarium
6 tepidarium

Caldarium

Natatio

300 RF

100 METRES

Plate 47 General plan of the Baths of Caracalla, reproduced from Amanda Claridge, *Rome-Oxford Archaeological Guide* (Oxford, OUP 1998).

Cisterns

Gardens

A Stadium
B Library
C Steps to the Aventine Hill

300 RF

100 METRES

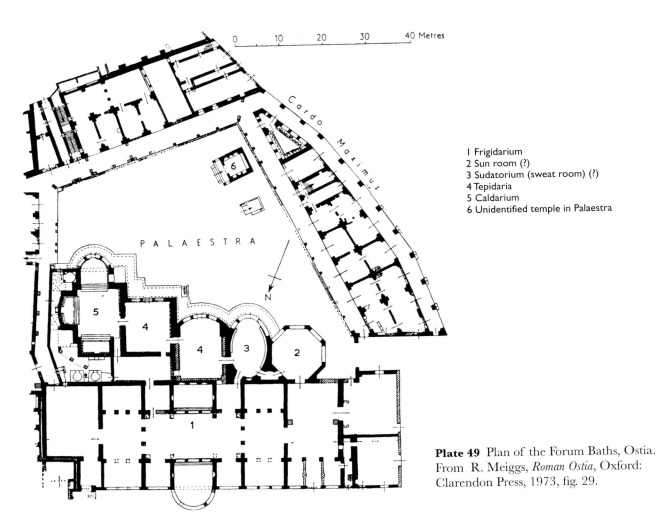

1 Frigidarium
2 Sun room (?)
3 Sudatorium (sweat room) (?)
4 Tepidaria
5 Caldarium
6 Unidentified temple in Palaestra

Plate 49 Plan of the Forum Baths, Ostia. From R. Meiggs, *Roman Ostia*, Oxford: Clarendon Press, 1973, fig. 29.

Plate 50 Reconstruction of the Mosaic of the Athletes from the Baths of Caracalla, Museo Gregoriano Profano, Rome. Photo: Vatican Museums. Neg N.XXXV.4.59/1.

Plate 51 Sculptural group known as the 'Farnese Bull', in the Museo Archeologico Nazionale of Naples.
Photo: Alinari Archives/Bridgeman. Reproduced with the permission of Ministero per i Beni e le Attività Culturali.

Plate 52 Forum of Augustus and Temple of Mars the Avenger. Photo: Fototeca Unione, AAR Photographic Archive, Rome.

Plate 53 Reconstruction of caryatids and upper storey of Forum colonnades. Photo: Fototeca Unione, AAR Photographic Archive, Rome.

Plate 54 Reconstruction drawing of niche, with statue and inscription, from Paul Zanker, *Forum Augustum: das Bildprogramm*, Tübingen: Wasmuth, 1968, fig. 33; from Degrassi, *Inscriptiones Italiae*, XIII. 3, Rome, 1937. © Ernst Wasmuth Verlag, D-72072 Tübingen, Germany.

Plate 55 Colossal statue of Mars. Capitoline Museum, Rome. Photo: Maria Teresa Natale, Rome.

SIC · ROMAE · EX · MAR
MORE · SCVLT,
PIRRHI · REGIS · MACÆDONIÆ · IMAGO,
Epirotarum :

Plate 56 Drawing of colossal statue of Mars, after E. Tormo, Francesco da Olanda, 1940, fol. 27, from Paul Zanker, *Forum Augustum: das Bildprogramm*, Tübingen: Wasmuth, 1968, fig. 48. © Ernst Wasmuth Verlag, D-72072 Tübingen, Germany.

Plate 57 Relief of Tellus, Carthage. Louvre, Paris, inv. no. 1838. Photo: © RMN/© René-Gabriel Ojéda.

Plate 58 Relief of Tellus, Ara Pacis, Rome. Photo: Alinari Archives, Florence.

Plates 59 and 60 Painting of Aeneas and Romulus from façade of house/fulling shop in Pompeii (IX.13.5), from Vittorio Spinazzola, *Pompeii alla luce degli scavi nuovi di Via dell'Abbondanza*, Rome, Libreria dello Stato, 1953, vol.1, figs. 183 & 184. L.R.300.d.9 vol. 1 fig. 183 & 184. By permission of the British Library.

Plate 61 Parody of Aeneas group, Stabiae. From *Bolletino d'arte* 35 (1950), 109, fig. 2. By permission of the British Library P.P.1931.plc.